THE SCIENCE OF HISTORY

SCIENCE ON VIKING EXPEDITIONS

by Isaac Kerry

T0020645

CAPSTONE PRESS
a capstone imprint

Published by Capstone Press, an imprint of Capstone
1710 Roe Crest Drive, North Mankato, Minnesota 56003
capstonepub.com

Copyright © 2023 by Capstone. All rights reserved. No part of this publication may be reproduced in whole or in part, or stored in a retrieval system, or transmitted in any form or by any means, electronic, mechanical, photocopying, recording, or otherwise, without written permission of the publisher.

Library of Congress Cataloging-in-Publication Data is available on the Library of Congress website.
ISBN: 9781666334692 (hardcover)
ISBN: 9781666334708 (paperback)
ISBN: 9781666334715 (ebook PDF)

Summary: Vikings were fierce warriors who sailed the seas looking for new lands. They were expert sailors and shipbuilders. Find out the science behind their explorations, shipbuilding, and daily life. Discover how modern technology is being used to discover more about the lives of Vikings and their expeditions.

Editorial Credits
Editor: Erika L. Shores; Designer: Heidi Thompson; Media Researchers: Pam Mitsakos and Jo Miller; Production Specialist: Tori Abraham

Image Credits
Alamy: Art Directors & TRIP, 43, Cindy Hopkins, 32, Danita Delimont, 44, GL Archive, 25, Graham Mulrooney, 21, Heritage Image Partnership Ltd, 19, Juniors Bildarchiv GmbH, 17, Universal Images Group North America LLC, 8; Getty Images: duncan1890, 5, GeorgeBurba, 22, Jeff J Mitchell, 39, Lorado, 29, nyiragongo, 18, Thos Robinson, 15; Newscom: akg-images249638, 27, ZUMA Press/Solberg, Trond, 23; Science Source: CLAUS LUNAU, 33; Shutterstock: brichuas, 20, Dawid K Photography, 34, Design Projects, 13, Elena Sherengovskaya, 31, Fancy Tapis, 6, GenOMart, 11, Igor Shoshin, 35, Ihor Kontsurov, 10, Kai Beercrafter, 36, KamimiArt (design element), Loco, 9, Lukas Pobuda, 38, Nejron Photo, Cover (Bottom), NERYXCOM, 30, Nick Fox, 41, Olinchuk, 7, PhotoVisions, 37, Russ Heinl, 45, Sergiy1975, 28, Stock image, 1, Stock image, Cover (Top)

All internet sites appearing in back matter were available and accurate when this book was sent to press.

Printed and bound in the USA. PO4882

TABLE OF CONTENTS

Words in **bold** text are included in the glossary.

CHAPTER 1

SAILING INTO THE UNKNOWN

A huge ship with a carved dragon on its front rises and falls with the waves. Bearded men strain against their oars. Horns blow and weapons are readied. A Viking raid is coming!

The years 793 to 1066 CE are known to historians as the Viking Age. During this time, the Vikings attacked places all over western Europe and Britain. They also launched many long-distance voyages. Some Vikings even made it as far as North America!

The Vikings did not have any advanced scientific knowledge. But their success as raiders and explorers depended on scientific **principles** and facts. Today, **archaeologists** and other researchers use their own scientific knowledge to study Vikings and their history.

Fact

The word *Viking* comes from the Norse word *víkingr*, which meant someone who journeyed for adventure.

5

WHO WERE THE VIKINGS?

By studying DNA gathered from archaeological sites, scientists learn about the origins of ancient people such as the Vikings. Research shows that Vikings may have started in the Scandinavian region. But as they expanded and settled new areas, they mixed with local populations.

What Is DNA?

DNA is essentially the "blueprint" for how the human body works. It is a chemical **molecule** in our bodies that contains our genes. Genes carry the information that determine how you look and how your body functions.

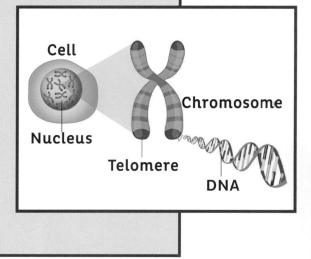

Cell

Nucleus

Chromosome

Telomere

DNA

Vikings came from an area in Europe known as the Scandinavian Peninsula. Today, it is home to Norway and Sweden. The country of Denmark is also part of this area. **DNA analysis** has shown scientists that the Vikings were not one specific group of people. People from different areas of the world usually have small differences in their DNA.

Raiding and exploring were not the main activities in Viking life. In fact, most Vikings were farmers. They grew crops such as oats, barley, and rye. They raised animals such as pigs, horses, and sheep. Winters were harsh. This meant farmers had to grow enough hay to feed their animals during the winter.

Most Vikings lived on small farms. In some areas the farms were near each other. They formed small villages. In others, the farms were more spread out.

Viking homes, called longhouses, often had grass roofs.

Crops need nutrients from the soil to grow. If the same field is planted each year, over time it will run out of nutrients. Vikings would slightly move where their fields were. This allowed their new crops to receive fresh nutrients from the soil.

Oats were one of the crops grown by Vikings.

LAND IN SCANDINAVIA

The many bays of the Scandinavian coast helped Vikings reach the ocean easily. Bays are an important feature for sailing. A bay is a section of water that is partially surrounded by land. This creates a calmer area of water. Boats can easily be launched into the water at bays.

The water in fjords is calm because big ocean waves do not reach it.

The coastline of Scandinavia is also dotted with **fjords**. These deep channels of water jut inland from the sea. They were formed millions of years ago by large bodies of slow-moving ice called glaciers. Having many different ways to get to the ocean made sailing and fishing easier. These activities were an important part of Viking life. In addition to fish, Vikings caught and ate other seafood such as eels, squid, and seals.

Refraction

Bays are calm because of a process called refraction. As waves from the ocean reach the shore, their energy is concentrated in different areas. In a bay, the parts of land sticking out into the ocean receive the high energy waves. The lower energy waves move into the bay. That means bays are ideal places for ships to be built and launched.

VIKINGS' SECRET WEAPONS

Vikings had the same weapons and strength as other people of the time. What truly set them apart were their longships. The ships usually carried about 60 warriors. Longships' speed and flexibility meant they could travel upriver as well as strike on the coasts. In addition, the light longships were able to be beached on land. Vikings could strike quickly and then sail away. Often a raid was over before any enemy soldiers had time to gather.

Fighting and battle were respected in Viking culture. Troops had high **morale**. Some evidence also exists of berserkers. They were Viking warriors who would enter a battle in a rage. These top warriors might have been put in the front lines to absorb enemy attacks. Untangling fact from fiction is difficult, but one thing is certain about the Vikings. They were known to be fierce fighters who terrified their enemies.

Fact

Berserker means *bear* and *skin* in the Vikings' language. Viking art shows warriors wearing animal skins into battle.

Vikings sailed the seas in their unique longships. The Viking Age marked a time when Vikings' power was feared around the world. But it wasn't when the Vikings, as a people, had their start. By the start of the Viking Age, Vikings had been making longships for hundreds, possibly thousands, of years. Longships were around 45 to 75 feet (14 to 23 meters) long. The front of the ships were carved to look like dragons.

Very few Viking longships have been found intact. So how can we know so much about them? One way is by using **experimental** archaeology. This field of study tries to reproduce ancient works. Scientists use only methods that would have been available in the past. They discover these methods by studying artifacts and piecing together ancient techniques. In 2012, a **reconstruction** of a Viking longship set sail. Studying it has helped scientists learn more about ancient ships.

Fact

Viking sails were most likely made from wool. To make enough wool for one sail, about 60 sheep needed to be sheared.

Scientists are still learning what made longships so special. One unique feature was how the **hulls** were made. Vikings built them using a technique called the clinker method. Pieces of wood that made up the hull overlapped each other. As a result, the hull was very strong. It also made the boat lighter and more flexible. Vikings used wood right after it had been cut down. This "green" wood was more bendable and easier to work with.

Longships' lighter weight meant they were faster than other boats. They could sail on rivers as well as the open ocean. Vikings used them to raid farther inland. They were also able to be carried across land if needed. No other people had boats like these.

Fact

The Vikings made another kind of ship called a knarr. It was a smaller boat used for trading.

The hull of a reconstructed Viking ship shows the way the wood overlaps.

RESEARCHING THE VIKINGS

One of the most important tools researchers use are primary sources. Primary sources are records made by people who directly took part in an event. Letters and speeches are examples of primary sources. Primary sources can also include objects such as artifacts or the ruins of villages. Viking sagas are a primary source used in studying the Vikings.

The ruins of a Viking settlement in Scotland

A saga in an ancient Viking text

Sagas were stories Vikings told about their gods, heroes, and voyages. There are also many that simply talk about everyday life. Scientists believe Vikings would tell these stories to each other out loud. Eventually they wrote them down.

Researchers have found the sagas very useful. Their stories about gods and monsters are too fantastic to be true. But studying what the sagas say about life in Viking times provide many clues about the past.

NAVIGATING WITHOUT A COMPASS

Some of the voyages the Vikings made were very long. The journey from modern-day Norway to Greenland is about 1,500 miles (2,400 kilometers). Keeping the same **bearing** is needed on long journeys. Going off course even a little bit can result in missing the destination. Today, sailors use compasses to find their way. Magnetic compasses were invented in China around 200 BCE. But they would not arrive in Europe until around 1200 CE.

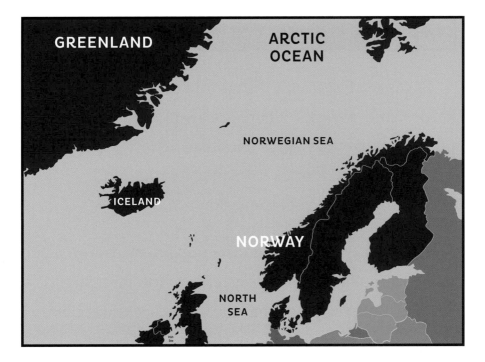

A wooden sun compass
used by the Vikings

    Vikings may have found their way by using a sun compass. A sun compass is a flat disk with a raised object in the middle. It can use the shadow the sun makes to tell direction. But what about when the sun was hidden behind clouds? Viking sagas tell of something called a sunstone. Scientists believe this might have been a special type of crystal. Crystals such as calcite stones make certain patterns when held up to the light. They can do this even when the sun is behind clouds.

Their ability to navigate let the Vikings go on long voyages. They started settlements in what is modern-day Britain and France. Sailing their ships led to discovering Iceland and Greenland. Two sagas, *Saga of Erik the Red* and *Saga of the Greenlanders*, spoke of their journeys to a place called Vinland. For years archaeologists debated where this land was.

Reconstructed buildings are at the site of the ancient Viking settlement in Newfoundland, Canada.

In 1960, Helge Ingstad, a Norwegian explorer, and Anne Stine Ingstad, an archaeologist, made a terrific discovery. On the shore of Newfoundland, in Canada, the couple found the remains of an ancient settlement. It took them at least five years to uncover the ruins. They discovered many artifacts and buildings built in the Viking style. This proved that Vinland was in North America. The Vikings were the first European people to discover the continent.

Anne Stine Ingstad and Helge Ingstad in 2014

CHAPTER 2

PILLAGE AND PLUNDER

Vikings are famous for their sailing and expeditions. They are equally infamous for their raiding. For most people in the Viking Age, seeing the sails of a longship would have been terrifying.

WHY GO RAIDING?

The first major recorded Viking raid happened in 793 CE. Vikings attacked a community of monks in England. The Vikings had existed for hundreds of years before this attack. The exact reason they started raiding is unclear. Scientists have done research and have come up with several ideas.

Researchers have used Viking sagas as well as other writings of the time to find an answer. These sources say that Viking men often had many wives. Scientists **hypothesize** that this led to a shortage of wives for young Viking men. Viking society put a focus on battle and courage. This led a Viking man to try to increase his importance to impress a future wife. He found fame and fortune through raiding.

Viking warriors thought raiding would earn them fame.

WEAPONS AND ARMOR

Most Viking weapons were made from iron. In the right conditions, iron can stay intact for thousands of years. The oldest iron artifacts date to 3200 BCE. Scientists today have many Viking weapons they can study.

Materials like wood break down over time. Many different creatures slowly eat away at it. In the case of wood, this is done by fungi, bacteria, and insects. But nothing is interested in eating metal!

So, what causes iron artifacts to break down? Most metals undergo a chemical process called corrosion. When iron is mixed with oxygen or anything wet, a process called oxidation happens. This chemical reaction changes the iron into iron oxide. Iron oxide is more commonly known as rust. Given time, rust will spread and destroy an entire piece of metal.

A rusty, ancient Viking sword was found at a burial site in Germany.

Luckily for scientists, Vikings were often buried with their weapons. These graves were fairly dry, oxygen-free environments. Corrosion was prevented to an extent. The result was many well-preserved artifacts to study.

Vikings used a variety of bladed weapons in battle. Axes were the most common. They were used by Vikings as weapons as well as tools. Almost any common Viking man likely owned an axe. A larger, two-handled axe known as the Dane axe was used by some warriors.

Richer Vikings often carried swords. A sword was seen as a status symbol. In addition to axes and swords, Vikings used spears and bows. Sometimes Vikings would throw a wave of spears as they charged into battle.

Fact

The pommel on a sword has two purposes. First, it helps to grip the blade. It also helps balance the sword.

Vikings were buried with their weapons because they thought they would need them in the afterlife.

Most Vikings fought with a shield. Animal skins covered the wooden shields and made them stronger. Because the shields were made from wood, not many examples remain today. But there are several images of them in Viking texts. Warriors would paint them with bright colors and designs.

Fact

Viking helmets probably did not have horns. This idea was made up later by artists. No horned helmet artifacts have been found.

Only the wealthiest Vikings had metal armor or helmets. The armor was usually chainmail. This armor is made from thousands of tiny rings locked together. It would usually be worn in a long shirt that came down to a warrior's thighs. Another type of armor was called lamellar. It was made by connecting small metal plates together. Vikings who could not afford metal armor used thick padded cloth to protect themselves.

An example of Viking armor

CHAPTER 3

VIKING LIFE AT HOME

It is important to remember raiding and exploring only took up a small part of Vikings' lives. Most of their time was spent farming. Other activities likely were fishing and trading. The seasons played a role in raiding trips. Usually, Vikings would raid in the summer so they could return in the fall and harvest crops.

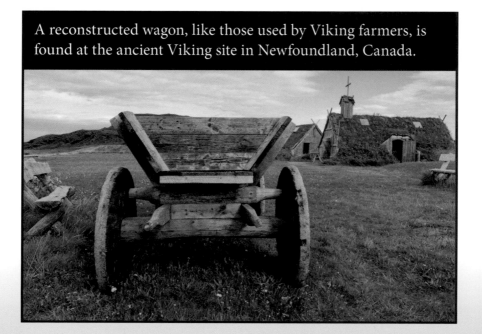

A reconstructed wagon, like those used by Viking farmers, is found at the ancient Viking site in Newfoundland, Canada.

Studying how Vikings farmed is difficult for scientists. Many early farming tools were made of wood. They have decomposed. However, clever researchers use information at dig sites to make discoveries. For instance, scientists examined specific scratches in the earth. It led them to believe farmers used a simple kind of plow called an ard.

Viking farmers used a wood plow called an ard.

Fact

Cattle were the most prized animal to the Vikings. Their word for money and cow was the same: *fé*.

VIKING DIET

Vikings ate a variety of food. Meat made up a major part of their diets. Pork, beef, and mutton were common meats. Vikings also ate horsemeat and various wild animals such as reindeer and elk. A main part of Viking meals was a thick meat stew called skause. It was left cooking over a fire for several days. New meat and vegetables were added each day.

A recreation of a Viking meal

Fish also made up the Viking diet. Fish were left out in the freezing air to dry out. This method can allow the fish to last for up to five years. Scientists have found Scandinavian fish DNA as far away as Germany. Vikings likely took dried fish along on their journeys.

Drying out fish kept it from spoiling.

FORGING IRON

Iron was incredibly important to the Vikings. Making iron tools and weapons was a complex process. It starts with iron ore. Iron ore is a form of mineral that can be turned into iron through a process called smelting. Smelting involves heating the iron ore to very high temperatures, sometimes over 2,012 degrees Fahrenheit (1,100 degrees Celsius). A chemical reaction then creates iron.

A recreation of Viking smelting

Scientists know bogs, such as this one in Norway, were a source of iron ore for Vikings.

Iron ore is usually taken from mountains. But Vikings had a different source that provided the metal: bogs. Bogs are wetlands made up of rotting plant matter called peat. Bogs are often formed by the lakes left behind by glaciers. Dissolved iron can wash into bogs from nearby mountains. Bacteria living in the bog turn the iron into small nuggets.

After iron was produced from the ore, Vikings could begin **forging** their metal weapons and tools. Men known as smiths were skilled in metalworking. They would heat iron in a forge. They then pounded the hot metal into shapes with a hammer.

What Is Steel?

Steel is a metal formed by mixing iron with **carbon**. Adding carbon to iron during the forging process changes the way iron crystals are arranged. The result is a much harder substance.

A piece of iron is pounded flat.

A scientist studies an ancient Viking sword.

Scientists discovered some Viking smiths may have accidentally made their weapons stronger. Excavations revealed the bones of the dead were sometimes taken from graves. Bones of animals and humans have been found at several forges. Scientists concluded that ground-up bones were added to iron. It is believed the Vikings thought this would give their weapons the strength of their ancestors. Adding these burnt bones to iron would have made a basic form of steel.

SETTLEMENTS

In addition to their homelands in Scandinavia, Vikings started many other settlements. Their voyages took them to Greenland, Iceland, and many parts of Europe. Scientists have taken artifacts from these settlements and discovered when they were built. They did this by using a process called carbon dating.

Many Viking settlements may have first started due to changing weather. If Vikings raided late in the year, winter weather would mean a much more difficult return voyage. Raiding parties "overwintered" in the areas they attacked. Over time these camps grew into more permanent settlements.

Carbon Dating

Carbon dating works by analyzing the properties of the element carbon. Over time parts of the carbon element decay at a set rate. Scientists can study this rate and use it to find out how old something is. Common sources of carbon are bones, wood, or other artifacts.

An ancient Viking settlement is located near mountains in Iceland.

Viking settlements provide scientists with some of their most important clues. Even though only the ruins of the settlement remain, many discoveries have been made. Scientists can look at the bases of buildings and discover how Viking settlements were laid out. Artifacts can be found in the ground, either accidentally dropped or placed as part of a burial.

Modern technology has provided researchers with new ways of locating Viking ruins. Many Viking buildings were made with wood and grass. They have not left any visible remains behind. But the plant life that grows over the top of ruins can look different from high above. By using satellite imagery, scientists can discover where these ruins are.

Fact

Satellites are launched into space. Cameras onboard take and send back detailed pictures of Earth.

A reconstructed Viking wood-frame house covered in grass in Iceland

The Viking Age ended nearly 1,000 years ago. Yet scientists are still discovering new and exciting facts about these legendary people. At the end of 2021, scientists discovered the exact date of the Viking settlement in Newfoundland. Previous estimates ranged anywhere from 793 to 1066 CE.

The Viking settlement in Newfoundland is called the L'Anse aux Meadows National Historic Site.

Scientists turned to an unlikely source for a more specific date. It was the sun. There is evidence that a huge solar storm hit Earth in the year 992 CE. It caused a surge in a certain kind of radiation. Knowing this information, scientists analyzed the trees that had been cut down at the Newfoundland site. They measured the amount of radiation in the tree rings. Then they were able to pinpoint the date the trees had been cut down: 1021 CE.

As scientific techniques advance, who knows what discoveries are possible? Even more secrets of the Viking Age are waiting to be unearthed.

An aerial view of three buildings at the L'Anse aux Meadows National Historic Site

GLOSSARY

archaeologist (ar-kee-OL-uh-jist)—a scientist who studies how people lived in the past

bearing (BAYR-ing)—what direction a ship is traveling

carbon (KAHR-buhn)—a chemical element that is found in all living things

DNA analysis (dee-en-AY uh-NAL-i-sis)—the study of the materials in cells to determine who they belong to

experimental (ik-SPEER-uh-muhnt-uhl)—relating to, based on, or used for experimenting

fjord (fee-ORD)—a long, narrow inlet of ocean between two cliffs

forging (FORJ-ing)—to heat metal in a special furnace

hull (HUHL)—the main body of a ship

hypothesize (hye-POTH-uh-size)—to create a hypothesis, or educated guess, about something

molecule (MOL-uh-kyool)—the smallest part of an element that can exist and still keep the characteristics of the element

morale (muh-RAL)—the feelings or state of mind of a person or group of people

principle (PRIN-suh-puhl)—a general or basic truth on which other truths or theories can be based

reconstruction (ree-kuhn-STRUHKT-shuhn)—the recreation or reimagining of something from the past especially by using information acquired through research

READ MORE

Romero, Libby. *Vikings*. Washington, D.C.: National Geographic, 2018.

Vallepur, Shalini. *People Did What in the Viking Age?* New York: Crabtree Publishing Company, 2020.

Yomtov, Nel. *Vikings: Scandinavia's Ferocious Sea Raiders*. North Mankato, MN: Capstone Press, 2019.

INTERNET SITES

10 Facts About the Vikings
natgeokids.com/au/discover/history/general-history/10-facts-about-the-vikings/

Britannica Kids: Vikings
kids.britannica.com/kids/article/Vikings/353900

Middle Ages: Vikings
ducksters.com/history/middle_ages_vikings.php

INDEX

ABOUT THE AUTHOR

Isaac Kerry is an author, stay-at-home dad, and firefighter. He lives in Minnesota with his wife, two daughters, and an assortment of four-legged creatures. He can often be found writing, wrangling children, or riding big red trucks. When not engaged in these pursuits, he loves reading, working out, and board games.